Beyond Chit-Chat

Sharing stories that matter to build deeper connections in faith communities

By Dave Daubert & Elaina Salmon

Copyright © 2022 by Day 8 Strategies

All rights reserved. No part of this publication may be reproduced, distributed, or transmitted in any form or by any means, including photocopying, recording, or other electronic or mechanical methods, without the prior written permission of the publisher, except in the case of brief quotations embodied in critical reviews and certain other uses permitted by copyright law. For permission requests, write to the publisher, addressed "Attention: Permissions Coordinator," at the address below.

Unless otherwise noted in the text, quotations from scripture come from the New Revised Standard Version Bible, copyright 1989, Division of Christian Education of the National Council of the Churches of Christ in the United States of America. Used by permission. All rights reserved.

Larger quantities of this book are available at a discount on our web site at www.Day8Strategies.com. For information on purchasing significantly larger orders, email the publisher at Resources@Day8Strategies.com for more information.

ISBN: 978-0991062140

Day 8 Strategies

1132 Morningside Dr.

Elgin, IL 60123

To contact the authors send an email to: Resources@Day8Strategies.com

Table of Contents

How to Use This Book	1
Introduction	3
Chapter 1: God the Story Creator	15
Chapter 2: Storyteller	27
Chapter 3: Story Listener	39
Chapter 4: Story Communities	55
Conclusion	69
Tactics for Moving Beyond Chit-Chat	75

How to Use This Book

Beyond Chit-Chat is a chance to look at how you are currently doing ministry in the congregational setting where you live and work. This book is written to help you do that work. The "you" in that sentence could be singular – you the reader reading and reflecting. But ideally the "you" in that sentence is plural – you working together as a group or even team of people. The best thinking about a future that is rapidly coming to us is rarely done alone. Each of us brings insights, questions and ideas to the table. Each of us bring blind spots and gaps as well.

That's why this book is written with a way for you to reflect, perhaps alone, but even more so, perhaps with others. After all, a book about sharing stories and changing what we talk about seems most useful if you talk! If you are using this book with a small group, a staff, a leadership team or your congregation's board, taking the book one chapter at a time will most likely work well for you.

At the end of each chapter is a section with materials for you to use. There is a scripture passage, questions for reflection or discussion, and a prayer. Of course, you can read and reflect using these alone, if you are reading the book by yourself. But the goal of these sections at the end of each chapter is to provide a simple framework to reflect on and discuss the content of the chapter you just read.

If you are using this book with a group, here are simple instructions for the work. Decide when and where you will meet. Be clear who is going to lead the discussion – easy to do since the questions are provided for you! Assign the section of the book that you will discuss and ask everyone to read the material prior to the meeting. Ask them to also be sure to look at the questions and ideas for reflection.

At the discussion session be sure everyone knows everyone. Read and discuss the scripture passage to open the formal time. Work through the questions. Each contains one or more questions to help you think about the content of the chapter and how it connects to your life and the work of the church in your setting. Close with prayer. There is a prayer to end each chapter's discussion, but we encourage you to also take time to share prayer concerns that are personally important to the participants as well. Be clear when the next session will take place, where it will meet, who will lead the discussion, and what you will discuss.

This kind of format it easy – you can do it. And it builds the chance for new insights, shared learning and the ownership of ideas that can help you not only think about this, but also actually begin to move forward! After all, a good book can be just the focus you need to get beyond chit-chat!

Introduction

We have all been in those places where conversations are shallow and don't reveal much – just chit-chat. But if you picked up this book, we assume you have an interest in stories and deeper sharing – getting beyond chit-chat. You probably would love to find ways to have more meaningful conversations and finding ways to develop deeper relationships and more authentic community.

And because this book is focused on how Christian faith communities are blessed by living in God's bigger story and how that includes each of us, we assume you have some desire to be immersed in stories within the life of a faith community – large or small — where you live out your faith. That's what connected the two of us as authors when we decided to write this. We both like stories and have seen and experienced the power that stories have to connect and transform in ways ideas simply can't do on their own. While chit-chat usually just fills space, really sharing meaningful stories can be a sacred and powerful thing! And many congregations have not taken advantage of shaping conversations to move toward deeper sharing and to telling meaningful stories with intentionality.

We believe that we all have a story worth telling and we are all worthy of having our story heard and honored. More specifically, we all have a faith story, and God, the great Story Creator, is both author and actor within each of our stories. This is a much broader story than what church we belonged to or what committee we served on. Our faith story is where and how we have encountered the God we meet in Jesus. It's the story of our life when we hungered for God's presence, when we heard God speak, when we wrestled with doubt, when God seemed silent and when the Spirit opened new possibilities beyond our imagination and carefully crafted plans.

Diana Butler Bass wrote the book *Freeing Jesus: Rediscovering Jesus as Friend, Teacher, Savior, Lord, Way, and Presence*. It is the story of her faith journey and where and how she met Jesus at each point along the way. At the conclusion, Bass defined her book as "memoir theology." "Memoir theology is the making of theology — understanding the nature of God — through the text of our own lives and taking seriously how we have encountered Jesus." (p. 264)

Diana Butler Bass is a religious scholar and prolific author, sought after speaker and columnist, with a doctorate in religious studies from Duke University. With a resume like that, we may be inclined to assume such storytelling is best done by an expert. Her stories help us see God in the unfolding of her life's events and through the people she encounters. Other expert authors like Frederick Buechner, Anne Lamott and Barbara Brown Taylor can inspire and transform us in similar ways.

But what about our story?

We have often met people who when asked about their faith story replied, "I don't think I have one." But when offered a few questions, space to reflect and the chance to speak, they discovered that they did indeed have a faith story. We all do. Memoir theology is not just for the religious scholar, prolific author or the expert. It is for each of us — for the 90-year-old man who sits in the last pew on the right side Sunday after Sunday and the 30-something young adult who is discovering how she lives out her faith in her job as a juvenile probation officer.

Even more, the work of memoir theology can be the life-giving work of faith communities where stories are told and received as the sacred texts that they are. Our faith stories nurture and build community and encourage us on our journeys of faith. Story communities build fellowship, spiritual formation, witness and proclamation around stories of faith.

As we move through this book, we will consider God as the Story Creator, give voice to the text of our own lives, turn to listen to our neighbor's story and look at ways to nurture storytelling and story listening cultures in our faith communities.

As people of faith, we are shaped by the biblical story, and more specifically, by the life, death and resurrection of Jesus. There's a lot in the Bible, but at its core, it is a love story between God and God's people. God, the Story Creator, started by breathing life into creation and then claimed a people, calling them to be models of righteousness and justice for all the world. When the people followed their own hearts and turned away, God kept the story going, working within it so that our story did not end in separation. Jesus came among us to reveal the heart of God, full of grace and truth, mercy and forgiveness. In Jesus, the Story Creator gave us a vision and a story of what God's coming kingdom would look like. That story of God's future reign shapes us for life and ministry today as we engage the world and seek to do justice, love mercy and walk humbly with God. God is weaving together a story that leads to life and forgiveness, love and hope, communion and beloved community.

The biblical story is not just ancient words for an ancient people. It is also a living word for us today. In our faith communities, we tell this story in Scripture, preaching, sacrament and song. Our life together centers on God's great love story — one which God continues to write and be immersed in. In community, as we tell our story and listen to the stories of one another, we hear how our lives are a place for God's continuing work.

Just as Diana Butler Bass did in her book about her journey, all of us are invited to listen to our lives and take seriously how we have met Jesus along the way. We are invited to tell our faith stories of when we felt God's nudge (or shove), when we heard Jesus' words spoken to us or when the Spirit moved to provide a new possibility when we had almost run out of hope. As the love story of Scripture is lifted off the page, we hear our stories reflected in the people of old. We see ourselves there in our brokenness, our longings, our grief and our joy; we hear God's response to our humanness — grace, mercy and love.

A living faith tells us that God does not just show up in biblical times or only in the lives of experts. God is at work in each of our lives — now! God, the great Story Creator, is both a writer and an actor in your story and as you live out your life, you are both a writer and an actor in God's story. Sometimes, we might be too busy or so barely tuned in that we are unable to sense and see God working or we struggle to see our lives woven in with God's. Yet, we are invited to listen to our life and discover God in its unfolding. How does our life speak? How is our life a place that reveals God's presence and love?

When we have done this work, we ask people in our congregations to turn to their neighbor and share where they saw God in the past week. Folks often squirm nervously in their chairs or look in the church bulletin as if the answer might be hidden there. Someone may even groan, but sure enough, people turn to their neighbor and begin a conversation that can feel awkward and imperfect at first. They might talk about what seems mundane, but we like to think that when they looked closely, they discovered God's presence in their story. Just as we did in ours. Just as you have done so in yours too.

Cultivating Holy Ground

These conversations can become holy ground. As we prompt people to share stories and as we make safe spaces for them to tell them, people discover that the mundane can suddenly become sacred. It takes at least two people for this to happen — the storyteller and the story listener. The teller needs the impetus to remember and to speak. The listener(s) provide the safe space and opportunity for this to happen.

What creates safe and sacred space is not just the presence of the story. It also involves the openness of the audience since every great story needs a great listener. As we think about storytelling and story communities, we need story *listeners* to make these two things work. Generous listening is one of the simplest ways we can answer Jesus' command to love one another. To listen to someone's story, deeply and intentionally, is one of the greatest gifts we can give someone. To be entrusted with someone's story, to hear a piece of their heart, is also one of the greatest gifts we can receive. The exchange of gifts in storytelling and story listening can be holy ground.

All this storytelling and story listening leads us to story communities. This is holy work suited for faith communities. We already share a sacred story — one centered in the life, death, and resurrection of Jesus. We are already drawn into life together. When we nurture a culture of storytelling and story listening, we are touched, transformed and inspired by God, an actor who is present in all our stories. We become witnesses to the incarnation — God taking on flesh in our lives. We become witnesses to resurrection — an unstoppable God who persists in working for life and love.

In the early church, this news of incarnation and resurrection was so exciting it spread like wildfire. The apostles told the story of Jesus and witnessed to the things they had seen and heard so that others came to believe. Knowing our faith story and when and how we saw God as an actor in our story is at the heart of our witness and our evangelism within and beyond the walls of our church.

Our bias and our assumptions are that stories have the power to change the world. There is so much that aims to disconnect us from ourselves and from each other. When people are what they produce, we easily dehumanize them to a mere commodity. When we draw lines between us versus them, we have hardened our hearts for battle. In a culture driven by social media, we share a curated and enhanced view of who we are and what we are feeling, often feeling miserable about ourselves as we compare our inner lives to the curated view of others. Furthermore, through social media, it's all too easy to hide behind an avatar or pseudonym and unleash our worse self on the world. We may not listen to others even though we think we do. With a simple click or setting, we can shut off, delete or filter out specific people or entire communities and their stories — beyond what may be appropriate or prudent. In the process, we solidify and embed the lines we have drawn between us and them.

But a story! A story humanizes the other and helps us reconnect with our own humanity. Stories connect us to one another, if for no other reason, to realize the deep longing we share to be heard. To be human is to love, grieve, fail, succeed, learn, be hurt and to hurt others. Stories remind us we are not alone in the struggle. Stories of simply being human give space for the messy, uncurated parts of our lives that reconnect us to ourselves. From there, our capacity for compassion and empathy grows. It is so much harder to harbor hate or anger towards someone once we know their story. It's so much harder to be us versus them when I see them in me. Stories connect and humanize us all and therein lies their power to change the world to a more just, kind, respectful and compassionate place. Faith communities are a natural place for this holy work to get started and be nurtured. Storytelling and story listening is one way we live out our baptismal call to "strive for justice and peace in all the earth."

We all have a story. We all have a story worth telling and we are all worthy of being heard and having our story honored. Our lifetime of stories is a place to see God as an actor in our story. Story communities offer the holy ground of storytelling and story listening. We can speak, we can listen, and together, we can encounter God's faithful presence. This is not just for our own sake; it is for the sake of a more just and compassionate world.

As you work through this book, we have a few points to help you get the most out of it. While we have voiced this introduction in "we" language, each of us as authors have taken lead roles in various places throughout the book. To include our stories (an important part of a book on stories), we have voiced the following chapters in first person using "I" language most of the time. This is because, like you, each of us have our own journey and our own stories to share. We'll usually tip you off as to which one of us is the storyteller.

We have also included a section for reflection and/or discussion at the end of each chapter. If you are reading alone, you may want to journal or reflect on these by yourself. If you are reading with a small group or a reading partner, take advantage of these to discuss ideas and share stories. Our goal is to help you not just read about storytelling but to involve you and your companions in the telling of them!

Finally, the last part of this book is a resource section — sort of a treasure bin of ideas. We hope when you finish reading that you are inspired to try things in your setting. We have shared several examples with instructions about ways you can increase storytelling in your setting and help your faith community become a more intentional story community.

So dig in and see what you find. It has been helpful for us to reflect and write this book. We hope you find it thought-provoking and helpful to read it!

For Reflection and Discussion

This book is designed to be read and reflected on – not just read and then shelved. So the scripture, questions and prayer below can be used for individual reflection by each reader. Even better, read each chapter in partnership with others and use the resources at the end of each chapter to foster a team discussion, a small group or other way to process and apply what you have just read.

Scripture

Now the birth of Jesus the Messiah took place in this way. When his mother Mary had been engaged to Joseph, but before they lived together, she was found to be pregnant from the Holy Spirit. Her husband Joseph, being a righteous man and unwilling to expose her to public disgrace, planned to divorce her quietly. But just when he had resolved to do this, an angel of the Lord appeared to him in a dream and said, "Joseph, son of David, do not be afraid to take Mary as your wife, for the child conceived in her is from the Holy Spirit. She will bear a son, and you are to name him Jesus, for he will save his people from their sins." All this took place to fulfill what had been spoken by the Lord through the prophet:

"Look, the virgin shall become pregnant and give birth to a son,
 and they shall name him Emmanuel,"

which means, "God is with us." When Joseph awoke from sleep, he did as the angel of the Lord commanded him; he took her as his wife but had no marital relations with her until she had given birth to a son, and he named him Jesus. (Matthew 1:18-25 NRSV)

Questions

1. Reflect on the Gospel of Matthew quote above. How does "Emmanuel" which means "God with us" impact your understanding of the biblical message? How do you experience Jesus as "God with us" in your life?

2. Reflect on this statement, "God, the great Story Creator, is both a writer and an actor in your story." What strikes you about this statement? How has it been true in your life?

3. When you are watching for God, what kinds of signs and actions are clues for you that what you are seeing might be God?

4. Where have you seen God in the past week? What made you think it was God?

5. Tell about a time you were entrusted with someone's story - what was that experience like? Now, think about a time when you entrusted someone else with your story – what was that like?

Prayer

God of creation, you are the author of life and also join us in the midst of it. Give us open hearts to receive your presence in our own lives and open ears to listen as others share their stories with us. Bless us with a desire to listen, share and discern in ways that enhance our lives and also build authentic community among us, for we come to you in the name of Jesus. Amen.

1

God the Story Creator

"And the Word became flesh and dwelt among us."

John 1:14

When my wife and I (Dave) got married, we gave each other a wedding gift. She got me a Bible. Inside the front cover she wrote our wedding vows.

The gift got my attention. While I already owned a Bible, receiving this one produced a new connection between my life's journey and Scripture. The world has changed since then. I have many Bibles in print, on my Kindle and on my phone, but the one I received when we got married sits carefully placed and visible on a shelf in my office — a sign of the place Scripture has in our lives and a reminder of how it has changed my life.

I have read that Bible so often that you can now easily tell where I have spent the most time in it. Yellowed pages and darkened edges show the wear of fingers and the marks of oils. You can see I read the New Testament more than the Old Testament. I read the Gospels, Acts and Romans the most. Eventually, the spine on the book broke at the Sermon on the Mount, one of my favorite sections of Scripture.

I still pull that Bible out from time to time, but the broken spine tells me the book had done its work and I don't want to send it to a book repair shop. There was something about the wear and tear that I want to preserve. The Bible was not only a gift of love from my wife, it also eventually became a record of one part of my faith journey and how I had spent my time in Scripture during that chapter in my life.

Something in the spiritual DNA that my wife brought to our relationship told her that a Bible was the right gift. Instinctively, she knew that as we were starting to write our own stories together, the bigger story of the God who has come to us in Jesus would set the context. Something deep within her knew that for our lives together to have the most meaning, our story would need to be tied to God's bigger one.

That simple truth is the grounding for this book. We all have stories that we live out. We all can tell them, but what gives life meaning is that each story in our life is also a chapter in God's bigger story. If we believe all our stories are just random moments but tied to nothing bigger, then we see life one way. But our lives find new connections and meaning that only God can give when we believe and see that God is up to something bigger and that each of our stories rests within that larger story.

Today my wife and I both want people to know the bigger story of God's love made real in the life, death and resurrection of Jesus. We want people to see the Bible as something important in their lives.

When someone we know has a new baby, my wife and I often want to give them a small gift. We may get them something cute to look at or something to wear, but we often also give them a children's Bible to go with it. Much shorter and more concise than the entire Bible, a children's Bible is really a book of Bible stories. It starts with creation and then walks through Scripture sharing particularly interesting and important stories along the way, usually with a scattering of stories from the Old Testament and then several from the life, death and resurrection of Jesus. It is our hope that these children will grow up to see their stories within the context of God's bigger story. Giving a young family a children's Bible is our gift to encourage the beginning of their journey.

Seeing Scripture as a story

As people of faith mature and spend more time in Scripture, they discover that these Bible stories in a children's Bible are not randomly bound in a book. We learn that these stories are all connected and are really segments of one larger story. The Bible is both a collection of stories and a compendium of material — all shaped by God who functions as the senior writer for a library co-written by a team of people inspired by God at work through the ages. It is designed to tell a bigger story.

This idea that Scripture is uniquely understood as story has given rise to the discipline called "narrative criticism" as a way of understanding the Bible. The term was first used by David Rhoads who wrote a groundbreaking book in 1982 entitled *Mark as Story: An Introduction to the Narrative of a Gospel*. In the ensuing years, hundreds of books and articles have explored the Bible as a whole and the story it tells. This approach to studying the Gospels, Acts and Revelation examines narratives with storytelling at their core and explores their characters, audience, contexts and themes. It has radically changed much about how people think, teach and preach from Scripture. This work has changed how we see and encounter God in the process.

A few years ago, the congregation I (Dave) serve used a Bible reading campaign that takes this concept of Scripture functioning as a larger, single story as its hook. *The Story* takes large excerpts from the Bible and then edits and arranges them to form a longer narrative. The text is formatted to look and read more like a regular book, a single column across the whole page with no chapter and verse numbers, so people feel more like they are reading a novel. People see creation in Genesis as the beginning. They read through the book and come to the New Jerusalem in Revelation as the ending.

Reading *The Story* is an experience to emphasize the unity of Scripture in telling God's one big and overarching narrative. As the people in the congregation read a section each week for 31 weeks, they saw the biblical story emerge and unfold as one long and continuous drama. Like all singular lenses on Scripture, this method has drawbacks, but using it helped people grasp the bigger picture and see the biblical story as something that functions as a whole.

The examples above remind us that whether we are sharing Scripture with young children or helping adults find their way through what is sometimes overwhelming, helping people see the Bible as a story helps them begin to make sense of it. Scripture emphasizes God's commitment to completing the story as God ushers in the reign of God. It is a book about an unfinished story within which we all live. And it is a book about a story whose ending is life-giving and secure because of the life, death and resurrection of Jesus.

Seeing Scripture in this way, unlike many other books of stories, tells us where we are going and offers encouragement and hope to trust that we will actually get there. Unlike most books, Scripture is both complete and incomplete. It uses powerful metaphors to share the beginning and the end in ways that capture our imagination and help us stand in awe of the God who is behind it all. Scripture gives grounding and fosters confidence for those who immerse themselves in it.

A story that is still being written

One unique thing about the Bible is that it shares a story whose middle is still being written by the narratives of our lives. The biblical story shapes our lives and the worldview through which we make sense of the world. At the same time, Scripture's images are not primarily a clear blueprint for the story as much as they serve as markers on the horizon. We take the hope we are given and then we journey into the promised reign of God that contains a lot of mystery along the way. There is a unique mix of clarity and ambiguity that the Bible offers us — we are encouraged to live into the mystery trusting that God will be there each step of the way.

With a God who works this way, it is no accident that the beginning of Scripture in Genesis is grounded in words that create the world which we and God share. God, as the Story Creator, speaks creation into being. God is the narrator and creation unfolds as God says, "Let there be...". The six days of creation are lived out as reality mirrors the stage directions of the narrator. Then Adam and Eve give more specificity to the human story. The big story includes lots of smaller stories — chapters in a huge yet unfinished narrative. And because creation is God's story, creation's history unfolds as God's memoir that conveys the events and relationships involving both God and those whom God has made.

This is why the narrative character is at the heart of Scripture. While it does eventually find its way to paper and then to digital mediums, it is oral and aural at its core. Whether the story is spoken or written, heard or read, it is God's way of making life happen in our temporal world. When eternity enters the temporal, it immediately becomes a story.

Since God speaks the story into existence and then speaks each of us into being as well, we quickly find ourselves in the narrative. It becomes our way of shaping our own stories while also participating in God's even bigger story. God's speaking sets the story in motion, and our lives contribute to the story in some way. Telling the story, especially when we see and include God in our telling, helps us discover who we are in the process. Stories shape us and provide meaning and perspective.

A story for a community

This shaping and meaning are not just or even primarily for individuals. Stories of creation, Abraham and Sarah's family tree, the Exodus, the times of the judges and then the kings of Israel all shape the Jewish people. Their call to be committed to the covenant at Sinai was uttered with the reminder from God that, "I am the Lord your God, who brought you out of the land of Egypt, out of the house of slavery; you shall have no other gods before me." In other words, identity and calling are all grounded in the shared story of a God who liberates God's people from slavery and then calls them to live out a new identity in response. To be connected includes sharing a common narrative, and to be a person of faith is to live within a shared narrative which admits its dependence on God.

When the actions of God's people don't match the vision God has for them, prophets are raised up. The prophet's role is to remind the people of their shared identity and urge them to get back on track so that their lives can contribute to rather than distract from the story God is writing in the world. God is willing to let us have meaningful involvement and freedom in the work we share, but God is not complacent when we get off track to a degree where the main themes of the story get lost. God reminds us of what our role is and calls us back to it when we stray too far from the center of the plot — like a good movie director.

God's collective claim on people is for the purpose of assembling a cast of characters who will live out the story well enough to draw others into it. It is a calling to be a particular kind of character in the mix of humanity. The cast is ever-growing, and God is always willing to write new players into the plot.

God enters the story

What makes the Story Creator unique is the commitment to go beyond merely constructing a drama that others will live out. God is more than a movie director. God is relational and sees creation not as an object to be viewed from a distance but as something to be loved and to be immersed in. So, God's authorship includes being the central figure in the story. Karl Barth makes the case that this is not a plan B simply because the story isn't unfolding well. Barth emphasizes that God started the story with the clear intent to enter it right from the beginning. A God who is "spirit and truth" also desires and commits to being "flesh and blood" as part of creating the tangible world in which we live. This is the mystery of the incarnation — that God joins us in the story and takes on the central role in the life, death and resurrection of Jesus.

Encountering God in the crucified and risen Christ means that we now not only see the results of God's authorship, but we also meet the author in the midst of the drama. The Story Creator is not detached from the story in a distant, third-person way. God is immersed within it and even subject to the same creation that God spoke into being from the beginning. Indeed, to be physical and to know a God who is spirit can only be fully done if God takes on the physical with us. The only way people can know a God "who no one has seen" is for that same God to join them in their stories and become seen and known in Jesus.

The story character of faith is also seen in Jesus who demonstrates the centrality of stories by telling them often. In fact, Jesus usually answered a question with either a question to make the questioners articulate their own answers or with a story, to help the questioner see the answer within a narrative instead of as just an idea. For Jesus, the ideas worth knowing impact how we live together and behave toward each other. In other words, a question that doesn't find its answer in the plot we are living isn't that important anyway. And any idea that is important enough to know, needs to be seen lived out to have any real meaning for us. So stories are a primary vehicle for Jesus' teaching because all good teaching is eventually woven into the story.

For example, when asked by a testy member of the audience, "and who is my neighbor?" Jesus replied, "A man was walking down the road from Jerusalem to Jericho and fell among thieves..." He then told the story of the Good Samaritan. When he was done, to see that the story had done its work, Jesus asked a question about the plot and the characters in it. He asked, "Which one was neighbor?" The man who asked the question understood the story well and the story had cornered him with a truth he was hoping to avoid. He answered Jesus' question correctly — the story had done its work without argument, force or confusion.

Such direct and clear work could never have been done with a teaching using a principle and an ensuing debate at the conceptual level, but within a story, a debatable truth became obvious and clear. Jesus would do the same thing again and again with stories about a sower who went out to plant seeds, a woman who had lost a coin, a father who waited expectantly for a wandering son, and on and on and on. In so doing, Jesus shows us a God who can't be easily understood using concepts, but who can be seen at work within a narrative.

All of us who want to help people know God would do well to remember this way of being with others. In a world divided by people who debate ideas, being people of stories which are shaped by Jesus may be a way to hear one another and be heard by others. Ideas are debatable, but stories work in ways that demonstrate and place into context concepts and truths rather than simply trying to explain them.

In addition, because Jesus is a character within the story that God is writing, he shows us what God wants us to see and be within the story. Rather than just saying, "Be like this...",

God shows us and calls us to be transformed and shaped through the imagery.

This means that God is also using stories to inspire us as characters within that story to a better understanding of life and creation. They shape and change us so that we are more able to participate in ways that make our lives meaningful contributions to that same story. Stories start the process, shape the process and are the result of the process — all at the same time!

There is an invitation and gift set before us. As we learn the biblical story, we gain a deeper understanding of the God who is the author of life and we see God's unfolding story in our daily lives. We can help people meet Jesus, and in doing so, know the stories God is writing and meet the one who is behind all the stories. We'll all be drawn into the ongoing drama of God's work and see ourselves being invited to participate in the story as it unfolds — an invitation and gift, indeed.

For Reflection and Discussion

As you finish this chapter and reflect, use the resources below for personal reflection or, even better, to discuss this material with others in a team or small group.

Scripture

But Mary stood weeping outside the tomb. As she wept, she bent over to look into the tomb; and she saw two angels in white, sitting where the body of Jesus had been lying, one at the head and the other at the feet. They said to her, "Woman, why are you weeping?" She said to them, "They have taken away my Lord, and I do not know where they have laid him." When she had said this, she turned around and saw Jesus standing there, but she did not know that it was Jesus. Jesus said to her, "Woman, why are you weeping? Whom are you looking for?" Supposing him to be the gardener, she said to him, "Sir, if you have carried him away, tell me where you have laid him, and I will take him away." Jesus said to her, "Mary!" She turned and said to him in Hebrew, "Rabbouni!" (which means Teacher). Jesus said to her, "Do not hold on to me, because I have not yet ascended to the Father. But go to my brothers and say to them, 'I am ascending to my Father and your Father, to my God and your God.'" Mary Magdalene went and announced to the disciples, "I have seen the Lord"; and she told them that he had said these things to her. (John 20:11-18 NRSV)

Questions

1. John 20 tells us that Christianity began when people like Mary Magdalene encountered the risen Christ and then went and told others their story. How is the story of Jesus shared in your community of faith? Where are people most likely to tell each other about their encounters with God?

2. Tell the story of your Bible. Where did it come from? Was it a gift? How have you used it? Where does it live now?

3. In one minute, tell the overview story of the biblical message. As you remember it, take us from Genesis to Revelation in broad but clear strokes (remember, you only get 60 seconds!).

4. How does the Biblical story influence and shape your worldview? What are the most significant places where you see that the world is impacted by God's story?

5. Think about the characters you remember best in scripture and think of one you relate to most. Which biblical character(s) do you connect with and why do you seem to relate to them?

Prayer

Story Creator, your Spirit moved over the face of the deep and you spoke creation into being, beginning the life-giving story that still gives us life today. We thank you for not only shaping the story in which we live, but also coming in Jesus to be a part of it. Give us eyes to see you at work in the world around us and give us hearts to sense your work in our lives. In all this, help us to be thankful for all that we have received from you, for the sake of Jesus Christ, in whose name we pray. Amen

2

Storyteller

In the spring of 2021, I (Elaina) was doing research for an upcoming sabbatical. I had already chosen my sabbatical theme of storytelling and now I had to figure out what opportunities existed to explore this more deeply. Since I had previously worked with my co-author, Dave, I decided to call him to see what resources and trainings he could recommend. I knew he had a wide breadth of experience and was connected to people and opportunities across the country and church denominations. Dave willingly agreed to a Zoom call.

I explained my hopes and dreams for my sabbatical focused on storytelling. He said, "It's interesting that you say that. I am starting to write a book on storytelling." Dave went on to tell me what aspects of storytelling he had thought to include, his approach to writing and self-publishing, and other things.

I sat there stewing in my chair. He was writing the one book I thought I had in me to write. I started to imagine if I could pull off writing a book during my sabbatical and beat him to the punch, but I didn't know the first thing about writing a book. Learning that process seemed a sabbatical theme in itself. I was getting increasingly flustered as the book I wanted to write was being explained to me by someone else. I was going to miss my opportunity. Finally, not being able to contain myself any longer, I blurted out, "Dave, you're writing my book!"

Dave responded, "Well, do you want to write it with me?"

I recoiled, surprised at the invitation, and suddenly felt very sheepish. That is not what I thought would happen when I blurted out those words. Truly, I wasn't fishing for an invitation. But Dave was sincere. The conversation continued, but now with a new focus on how we could write the book together.

That night at the dinner table, I told my family about the opportunity. I relived every feeling as I told the story. They were, of course, very excited for me.

I told the story again a few weeks later to friends of ours. Again, I relived the feelings. My friend's eyes were wide and expression expectant as I told the story. But this time, I added, that it must have been the Holy Spirit that made me blurt out, "Dave, you're writing my book!" I don't think I would have said it without a shove from the Spirit.

Now, over a year later, I am certain that the Spirit was moving to open a new possibility, even from the first inkling I had to give Dave a call.

Wendell Berry once said, "Telling a story is like reaching into a granary full of wheat and drawing out a handful. There is always more to tell than can be told."

What Berry wisely knew is that every story is rich and full. Important stories in our lives are the richest and fullest — there is always more to be found and explored. Every time we tell the story, even though we may feel like we know it well, we relive it and reconnect with it. This is often more than just in the recounting of the facts; we immerse ourselves in the story and reinvest ourselves emotionally in it as well. We discover new things about the story. We discover new things about ourselves.

Neuroscientists have monitored the brains of people as they tell stories. They see how various parts of the brain are energized as the story is told. What they have repeatedly found is that telling the story doesn't just give us a chance to recount the facts; our brains fire in much the same pattern as they did during the actual event. Telling a story not only helps us remember, in some ways, we genuinely relive the events.

The first person blessed by telling personal stories is often the storyteller. As the storyteller digs into a story, even a familiar one, the chance to use new words, expand one part of the story or another, and dig deeper means that the same story told again is often not the same story. It has grown, stretched, been embellished or changed in some other way. In the process, the storyteller is changed too.

Some stories last a lifetime

All of us have things that happen in our lives that, over time, we recognize as significant. We see them as impacting us in bigger ways. They are often stories of accomplishment, serendipitous joy and love. Or they may be stories of struggle, deep pain and loss. Within these events, we find hope, healing, reconciliation and meaning. It is within these events that we, as people of faith, often sense God acting most deeply in our lives.

In 2013 my wife and I (Dave) were blessed to have a sabbatical where we focused on Celtic Christian spirituality. After it ended, we were blessed with both an enriching experience that included a month of learning in Ireland and a hunger to learn more. We began to explore where we could gain more training in spiritual formation. After looking at several options, we enrolled in a certificate program at Columbia Theological Seminary in Decatur, GA.

The first class we took was taught by Diedre Rich, the director of the program. It was a foundational class and the introductory class that everyone was required to take before choosing electives and pursuing specific interests. An exercise that she had us do was a reflection on our life journey. We were asked to think about significant events in our lives where things were filled with joy and where we struggled. We were asked to reflect on people who had made a major impact on our lives and how they had done so. In each case, we were challenged to use God language and to share how we had come to see God involved in the events of our lives and relationships.

Diedre gave us time to make a timeline, reflect and fill in various chapters of our lives, and to think of the stories that were behind each of the events and relationships we had remembered. It took significant energy to do this work and she gave us what we needed to remember, reflect and think about the stories we would share with others. Then we split into small groups and shared the stories we had remembered and how God had been involved in them. It was more than an exercise; it was a chance to truly connect with other people — many of whom we had not known very well before we did this. The chance to share our stories, listen to the stories of others and discern how God had been involved was a powerful opportunity for all of us to grow deeper in our faith and closer to each other. As we divided into small groups and shared our stories and how we saw God in them, there was a connection that went well beyond people getting to know each other — we were sharing holy space.

A committed storyteller, a title which I hope all who read this will desire to claim, will spend time reflecting on their story and where and how they have seen God at work in it. As we listen to our lives and reflect on how God has been involved, we meet the Story Creator. Frederick Buechner puts it this way:

> I think our faith, if it's worth anything, comes from the story that each one of us has lived in this world, not just from what we heard from the pulpit. Our faith comes from our individual stories. It is through our stories that God speaks to us and gives us a sense that they have a plot.... It gives us all a clue that to remember far enough, to remember deeply enough, is to remember God, it's to remember Eden, to remember where you came from, and that through remembering you work your way back to some truth that is a liberating and healing truth. (The Remarkable Ordinary: How to Stop, Look, and Listen to Life, pp. 59, 64)

The stories of our lives become a revelation, and then as we tell our stories, they become a witness to the great Story Creator, a writer and actor in our stories. Stories of healing, reconciliation and restored hope offer a chance for the storyteller's story to open a window into life that may help others see God at work. A good storyteller isn't telling the story to say, "Look at me!" A well told story offers a chance to see beyond the teller into a wider holy space in which we are all somehow connecting with something deeper. Listening to our lives and knowing our own story opens up opportunities to share our stories in meaningful ways. When it is shared well, others feel blessed and inspired by the telling. In the process, holy space is created. It happens.

Telling a story creates space for others

Rowan Williams, former Archbishop of Canterbury, wrote about this kind of holiness in his wonderful little book, *Being Disciples*. In his chapter on holiness, he redefines holiness, pressing against the common moralistic notions that it is about what we don't do (smoke, drink, play cards, etc.). Instead, he refocuses holiness on when we are most like Jesus, doing what Jesus does. This often occurs in our connections with others and how we engage them. He writes, "They allow you to see not them, but God. You come away from them feeling not, 'Oh, what a wonderful person,' but 'What a wonderful world,' 'What a wonderful God,' or even, with surprise, 'What a wonderful person I am too.'" (p. 53)

One example of this comes from my life story about marriage. When I (Dave) was nineteen, I married a girl named Kelly. We were both in college and so school, part-time work and finances pulled us in a number of directions. By the time I graduated from college we had decided to split up.

I remember sitting down with my parents to tell them that we were getting divorced. I was nervous. It was the first time I had shared with them about the decision. In fact, in that moment, the anxiety of telling them was in its own way almost as stressful as the decision to divorce. But I shared it with them and of course, they loved me and were supportive in spite of my stress.

Over time, as I became more removed from the immediacy of that stressful decision, I became more comfortable talking about it. I eventually met Marlene, remarried and have been blessed now with almost forty years of a healthy and meaningful marriage. I feel no residual pain and have even found that I am grateful for the first marriage and the divorce and what they taught me about relationships, healing and grace. I am a better person and spouse today in many ways because of how that painful experience helped me see myself, other people, God and grace.

That means I can now talk about getting divorced without the anxiety I felt when I first told my parents all those years ago.

One Sunday several years ago, I mentioned being divorced and remarried in a sermon. It happened that I mentioned it on a Sunday when a newly married couple was visiting the congregation. The new husband had grown up in a conservative Christian tradition. He had married and then divorced. His church removed him from all leadership roles and deemed him unfit to hold any meaningful position in the church. The wife had grown up Roman Catholic. They found themselves outcasts in their own stories because he could no longer go to his previous church and he couldn't receive communion in the Roman Catholic Church because he was a divorced person.

They found their way into church on a Sunday when I happened to mention being divorced during the sermon. Imagine their joy when they found that in this church you could be divorced and still participate — even preach and preside at communion! It was what they needed to hear to find a pathway for their own story's next chapter. They joined the congregation and took on meaningful roles in the life of the church. Somehow, totally without any careful planning on my part, telling my story made them feel like they were going to be okay and they could step into a new beginning. God was not done with them yet. This is the kind of holy moment that a story can sometimes create.

Tender care of storytelling

In storytelling, we craft the story for the audience. Not all stories are told in the same way to everyone. How the audience relates to the story impacts what you can do as a storyteller.

For example, at one end of the spectrum is the airplane conversation. You find yourself in a seat on a plane next to a chatty person and end up in a conversation. As conversation topics come and go, various stories come to mind, and you share them with your seatmate. Because the person is from another state and has no connection to anyone, you can share the stories more openly. If you are telling a story about a co-worker named Bill, you might simply say, "I work with this guy named Bill...", and tell the story using his first name.

On the other end of the spectrum, you may be processing some stuff with a friend who knows Bill, and the story involves some difficult things about Bill. You may have to decide if it is even appropriate to share the story with this person since they know Bill. And if you do, you may need to leave out his name and a few contextual details so Bill isn't implicated in your story — to do so would be inappropriate.

The bottom line: be careful with the people in your stories. The more negatively a character looks as you share the story, the more careful you need to be, especially with people who may know the person. Your goal in storytelling, especially in the context of a faith community, is not to avoid negative stories — it can be important to share them. But it is also not the storyteller's job to shame or embarrass others as the story is told. Nor should a story share things in ways that reveal things, even good ones, that a person in the story would not want shared.

A good story that is well told is an amazing doorway into life and growth. A faithful storyteller will do well to use stories, whether they are about pain or celebration, to illuminate how life is experienced in ways that dig deeper without burying someone else along the way. When this is done well, stories reveal the most meaningful things about our lives but do it in ways that also enhance our lives as we journey together.

For Reflection and Discussion

As you finish this chapter and reflect, use the resources below for personal reflection or, even better, to discuss this material with others in a team or small group.

Scripture

The next day Jesus decided to go to Galilee. He found Philip and said to him, "Follow me." Now Philip was from Bethsaida, the city of Andrew and Peter. Philip found Nathanael and said to him, "We have found him about whom Moses in the law and also the prophets wrote, Jesus, son of Joseph from Nazareth." Nathanael said to him, "Can anything good come out of Nazareth?" Philip said to him, "Come and see." (John 1:43-46 NRSV)

Questions

1. As you read John 1:43-46, what about sharing faith and stories stands out for you in the lesson? How did the fact that Philip and Nathanael shared a common scriptural base enhance their interactions?

2. What is God like? List ten or more words that describe what is most important to you about God.

3. Use the words you listed in two to think of stories where these things have happened in your life. How does using these words about God impact how you see these events? Pick a word and journal about it if you are alone or share a story with others if you are reading this in a group.

4. Tell a story about a time when the Holy Spirit opened up a new possibility for you.

5. Think of a story of a significant moment in your life. Meditate on that story. Recall the setting, your feelings, who was present with you, the events as they unfolded. What evoked the greatest energy? What was the turning point? Now consider what ways God felt present. Did you realize it then or now in retrospect?

Prayer

Story Creator, you are the author of life and the giver of each day. So, we begin by saying thank you for the gift of life. Yet we thank you all the more that in Christ you have come to share in that life as well. We rejoice in your presence and pray for eyes to see you at work among us. And we pray for the Word that has become flesh to shape the words of our lives, that we may both see our story as part of your bigger story and share our stories in ways that share and shape life, for the sake of the Word which became flesh, Jesus Christ, our Savior and Lord. Amen

3

Story Listener

Craig and Molly had come from out of state for an overnight visit. I (Elaina) am sure that on Friday night we had pizza (because we always ate pizza when we were together) and I am sure the evening was filled with laughter. Yet, what stands out in my memory is sitting around the table on Saturday morning. I had made baked oatmeal and a large pot of coffee. The kids were off playing while Craig and Molly and my husband, Shawn, and I lingered around the table lounging in our flannel pajama pants and sweatshirts.

Craig's mom had passed away in the previous year and I asked him about what had happened. Craig and Molly shared the story of her cancer, how she faded away. They told of the travel between Muncie and Indianapolis to care for her and saying good-bye. They cried at points as they told the story of their loss and grief. Shawn and I had tears in our eyes too. Occasionally, Molly would reach over and gently rub her hand over Craig's shoulder. There were moments of silence until the next words were ready to be spoken. For Shawn and me, there was nothing to say that could fix the sadness, so we just listened and bore witness to their experience.

That morning together was profoundly holy. I trust that Craig and Molly felt loved and cared for, and Shawn and I felt the humble privilege of being entrusted with their story. In the grief, there were moments of beauty and love. Our friendship and connections were nurtured and deepened. Around the breakfast table we met God in the story, in the relationship and in the vulnerability of being human. In the process, we shared in the hope we hold on to as we walk through the valley of the shadow of death.

It is a gift to be heard, to have your story listened to and honored. There are also gifts to be received in listening. This is holy work.

Listening as an act of love

David Isay, the creator of StoryCorps, says "listening is an act of love." StoryCorps provides people from across the country the opportunity to record and preserve the stories of their lives. This is accomplished in an interview format between two people who know each other. In a StoryCorps booth, the interviewer has 40 minutes to ask questions and collect key stories from someone who is important to them. Isay encourages people to approach the interview as if it's the last forty minutes you have with someone before death, and for many people, it becomes one of the most important times of their lives, both for the storyteller and the story listener. At the conclusion, those involved get an audio recording of the interview and a copy is sent to the Library of Congress. After eighteen years of StoryCorps, Isay affirms that listening is an act of love because it affirms that the speaker's life matters and that their story and experience is worthy of being heard. ("David Isay—Listening as an Act of Love." On Being podcast.)

In our Christian life, we are called to such acts of love. Jesus' final commandment to the disciples was that they love one another. It is the command we hear on Maundy Thursday, when the church remembers Jesus washing the disciples' feet and sharing the last supper with them. As Jesus' death looms large, he gives parting words to his friends, arguably the most important words that he has shared:

> [Jesus said,] "A new command I give you: Love one another. As I have loved you, so you must love one another. By this everyone will know that you are my disciples, if you love one another." (John 13:34-35)

Most of the time, I doubt we imagined that living out Jesus' command could look like good listening. We may think of noble and generous things like feeding the hungry, tutoring at-risk children, protesting injustice, visiting the homebound or imprisoned, or taking meals to a friend who is sick. Without a doubt, those are acts of love that give life to Jesus' command. Good listening may seem insignificant compared to those acts of service, but if you recall a time when you felt deeply heard, a time when your story was honored, you know the power of love experienced when someone listens well.

Most people love to be listened to. As we get to tell our stories, the essence of who we are is revealed. Our experiences, feelings, heartbreaks and hopes are uncovered, and we become more deeply known. To be deeply known — both in our beauty and in our brokenness — is part of our healing and wholeness. Yet, that can also feel vulnerable. We might wonder, if someone knows who I really am, will they reject me or love me? Yet, love and connection grow as we share our lives and risk vulnerability. When I see that beauty and brokenness lives in you, I know all too well that it also lives in me, and I feel a little less alone. Listening is an act of love. At its best, it opens doors for connection, truth and love.

In *Life Together: The Classic Exploration of Christian Community,* Dietrich Bonhoeffer writes,

> The first service that one owes to others in the fellowship consists in listening to them. Just as love of God begins with listening to His Word, so the beginning of love for the brethren is learning to listen to them. It is God's love for us that He not only gives us His Word but also lends us His ear. So it is His work that we do for our brother when we learn to listen to him. Christians, especially ministers, so often think they must always contribute something when they are in the company of others, that this is the one service they have to render. They forget that listening can be a greater service than speaking. (p. 97)

Years ago, my friend Kathy and I traveled together to a clergy conference. On the flight home, my introverted soul was done with people. I took the window seat, curled up a blanket as a pillow, turned my back to the world and tried to sleep. Kathy, however, started chatting with the two men across the aisle. She invited them further into their story by asking good questions and staying curious. The two men started to come alive as they got to share more about their work and their lives with someone so willing to listen! The three of them had a lovely flight home while I was trying to sleep away my grumpiness. I am willing to bet that those two guys loved being listened to and that they went home that day feeling assured that their life mattered. What a gift Kathy had given them.

Listening, even though it is a basic life skill, is an act of love. Generous listening is one way we live out Jesus' command to love one another. Just as we are all capable of telling a story well, we are all capable of listening well too. It just takes some practice.

Communication 101

When Craig and Molly shared their hearts that Saturday morning, I was a good listener. Maybe at my best. I was present, I did not have an agenda and I offered space for them to speak and silence for reflection. I did not jump in to fix anything and did not offer any cliches about death that would do more harm than good.

However, I am not always a good listener. I am often distracted by a list of things to do or the buzz of my phone notifications. Sometimes I am preoccupied by my agenda or I am trying to discern the agenda of the speaker. Beauty and brokenness exist in all of us.

A good listener, though, is part of what makes a good story. I have had the experience of bad listeners who close their eyes while I am talking, who are looking over my head to see who else is in the room, or who glaze over with a faraway look as I am speaking. All too often, people listening to us are more engaged by the notifications on their cellphones. In those experiences, the story gets shut out and shut down. Why bother sharing if I do not think a listener is paying attention? An ineffective listener communicates that what I am saying really doesn't matter which quickly gets interpreted internally as I do not matter. But a good listener, who is engaged, present and giving every cue that they are listening and interested, invites a story to be told with more depth, more detail and more feeling. A good listener helps make a good story!

At the same time, a good listener doesn't over engage in ways that take over the story. Interruptions can derail the storyteller and even squelch the spirit. I (Dave) grew up in a family and culture where we learned to talk over each other. We even learned to listen fairly well as we did it. But it wasn't good practice and it wasn't easy to find your way in from the outside. When I got married to Marlene, she found herself overwhelmed when we visited with my family. There was little space for her to find her way in to share her stories.

Marlene shared this frustration with me and helped me see how hard it was to be heard. I have learned to run interference for her when we visit my family, so she has more space to participate (sometimes). In the process, I have learned to listen better, make space for people more intentionally and to interrupt less in other settings too. I am still a work in progress, but I am also living proof that we can all get better at this if we work at it!

So, to be clear, effective listening is an act of love. Ineffective listening has the opposite effect.

Good listening is more than just staying quiet while someone else talks. Yep, read that again. Good listening is an art and commitment that requires practice.

Already we have identified qualities of effective and ineffective listening. If in reading this, you thought about a story when you felt deeply heard (or when you did not feel deeply heard), you have already started to identify these qualities yourself. Good listeners practice:

- making eye contact
- not interrupting or derailing a story to tell their own
- allowing silence for reflection
- reflecting back to the speaker the emotions they are hearing
- asking good questions that allow for the speaker to hear their story more deeply or clearly
- refraining from trying to fix things or offering unsolicited advice

Some of this is Communication 101. Yet, as we have experienced both as the storyteller and story listener, effective listening is not always practiced. We all face major roadblocks to being effective listeners.

Practicing presence

One of the biggest hurdles to effective listening is a world full of distractions and busy minds. Every day has a list of demands and a schedule to keep. Our phones beep and ring with calls from work, weather alerts, news updates, social media notifications and messages from the dance team, scouts, the school, doctor's office and bank. No wonder it is hard to be in the moment! Perhaps you remember the dog from the Pixar movie, Up, who will be in the middle of a sentence and suddenly get distracted by a squirrel. Every time, his head turns abruptly and he shouts, "Squirrel!" We might have a squirrel problem too.

To be a good listener is to be present in the moment and with the speaker. That takes work and intentionality on our part as the listener. When we find ourselves distracted, these practices can pull us back to the present:

- Simply name five things you can sense in the encounter.
- Take three deep breaths (then more as needed).
- Bracket the distractions and put them aside until they can receive their rightful attention later.

Good questions

When a story listener asks a question, it communicates that they are tuned in and interested in what the storyteller is saying. An effective listener can help draw out a story with good questions. A little curiosity can go a long way, but the best curiosity is as much for the storyteller's sake as for the story listener's. Sometimes there's a story that wants to be told, and open, honest questions can help someone discover their own feelings, truth and wisdom.

Both authors have had the opportunity to experience the Quaker tradition of *clearness committees* on a few occasions. In this practice, one person gets to present a question or issue. The members of the clearness committee then ask open and honest questions to help the speaker listen for their own inner wisdom. In this situation, good questions do not assume an answer or try to sneak in advice. Questions are for the speaker's sake and not for the listener's curiosity or to demonstrate the listener's expertise.

As we think further about good questions, we can tune into the storyteller's motive or desire. What is the storyteller longing for? Follow the emotions of the story. How did this experience make the storyteller feel? In a meandering story, what is the underlying story that longs to be told?

It's not about us

As I was thinking about when I am at my best as a listener, it is when little or nothing is expected from me in response. As Dietrich Bonhoeffer reminds us, often pastors think they must have something to say as their offering to a speaker. The internal pressure of having an intelligent, thoughtful, "Christian" response can derail any of us from just listening to the story and person in front of us. We can distract ourselves from being a good listener when we are too focused on figuring out what to say in response.

It is our effective listening and not our intelligent, thoughtful, "Christian" responses that can be the greater blessing.

One of my favorite books on storytelling and story listening is *Kitchen Table Wisdom: Stories that Heal* by Dr. Rachel Naomi Remen. Dr. Remen is a physician, professor of medicine, therapist and a long-term survivor of chronic illness. Her book offers a collection of true stories from her life and medical practice about the courage and wisdom people found in sharing their stories. She speaks to the power of effective listening.

> Listening is the oldest and perhaps the most powerful tool of healing. It is often through the quality of our listening and not the wisdom of our words that we are

> able to affect the most profound changes in the people around us. When we listen, we offer with our attention an opportunity for wholeness. Our listening creates sanctuary for the homeless parts within the person. That which has been denied, unloved, devalued by themselves and by others. That which is hidden.
>
> In this culture the soul and the heart too often go homeless.
>
> Listening creates a holy silence. When you listen generously to people, they can hear truth in themselves, often for the first time. And in the silence of listening, you can know yourself in everyone. Eventually you may be able to hear, in everyone and beyond everyone, the unseen singing softly to itself and to you. (Kitchen Table Wisdom: Stories that Heal, pp. 219-220)

The act of listening is powerful. We often simply need to let go of our preoccupation with getting our responses right.

There are several storytelling formats that take this pressure off. In contemplative listening practice, participants each take a turn sharing their truth or a response to a question or prompt. When a speaker is done, all participants sit in silence to honor the person and words spoken. No one gives a spoken response at all. The group holds space for each person's story to be told and truth to be spoken.

In group spiritual direction, holy silence is offered again, but in this case, participants are listening for the Spirit's response to the speaker's reflection. Listeners, then, offer a response that is guided by the Spirit.

In other more secular story circle practices, listeners offer a simple "thank you," after someone shares their story.

Each of these story sharing formats, help listeners listen and receive a story as a gift. We can also learn from these formats of ways to listen more deeply in our one-on-one conversations. We can put aside the worry about figuring out our response or the anxiousness we might feel to fill the silence. Sometimes, simply thanking someone for sharing their story and their heart is enough to honor the exchange. It's not about us; it's about the storyteller.

The danger of a single story

Another way we can trip ourselves up in being a good listener is when we filter what is being spoken through our own expectations and experiences. This is when our stereotypes and prejudices get in the way. It's when we hear what we want to hear instead of what is being spoken or we think we know the substance of the story before it has been completed. Good listening includes listening beyond our expectations of who someone is, what we think they are going to say or what they are trying to say.

Nigerian novelist, Chimamanda Ngozi Adichie, in a 2009 TED Talk, shares about the danger of a single story. When she came to the United States, her university roommate had one single understanding of what it meant to be African. The roommate was surprised Chimamanda spoke English so well, even though English is an official language of Nigeria. The roommate imagined tribal music, but Chimamanda loved Mariah Carey. Certain that Chimamanda must have cooked over a fire, the roommate thought she would not know how to use a stove. The roommate had one single story and idea of what it meant to be African that was shaped by the stories of Africa as told by Americans — that it was a place of tragedy, with incomprehensible people, war and violence, poverty, AIDS and people waiting to be saved by a kind, white foreigner.

Chimamanda's story and that of her Nigerian family and friends was so much richer, varied and complex than this single story that shaped her roommate's perception of her.

In her TED Talk, Ms. Adichie says, "The single story creates stereotypes, and the problem of stereotypes is not that they are untrue, but that they are incomplete. They make one story become the only story."

If we are stuck with one story about the immigrant, the person who is experiencing homelessness, the drug addict, the Black Lives Matter activist, the police officer, the Muslim, the atheist, the Republican or the Democrat, we overlook the rich, varied and complex stories that shape each individual. Even more, we overlook our common humanity and the ways we may be more alike than different.

Effective listeners will make space in themselves and in their listening for more than a single storyline for each person. Then they can make space in community for stories and the people who are most often marginalized. This is an act of love. It's an act of love that helps create a more kind, just and compassionate world.

The tender care of stories

Finally, as story listeners we must care for the stories and the people who have entrusted their story with us. It is yet another aspect of listening as an act of love. When someone shares their story with us, they are sharing a piece of their heart. Their story is a sacred text in which their longings, hopes, disappointments, vulnerabilities and failures are revealed. It is no small thing to be entrusted with a story, and so we hold it with care and respect. A storyteller is the owner of their story and so they decide if, when, where and how their story is told. The stories confided to us are not ours to tell.

After I wrote this chapter, I reached out to Craig and Molly and asked them if I could share their story. I emailed them what I wrote, and they happily gave their permission. Craig expressed appreciation that I remembered him and this story with the same amount of detail as he did. In both of us recalling it, we once again experienced the sacredness of storytelling and story listening, the connection forged between our families and how we met God on our walk through the valley of the shadow of death.

For Reflection and Discussion

As you finish this chapter and reflect, use the resources below for personal reflection or, even better, to discuss this material with others in a team or small group.

Scripture

Beloved, since God loved us so much, we also ought to love one another. No one has ever seen God; if we love one another, God lives in us and his love is perfected in us.
God is love, and those who abide in love abide in God, and God abides in them. (1 John 4:11-12, 16b NRSV)

Questions

1. As 1 John grounds us in God's love, it also connects our love for one another to that same love. How do you experience God's love in community? Can you share a story of a time when that love really impacted you?
2. When have you felt deeply heard? What did that feel like? How did you know the other person was listening well?
3. What are your greatest challenges to being a good listener? Who is someone who has been a good listener for you and what do they do that makes them effective?
4. Tell about a time you were surprised by someone's story because it was different than what you expected.
5. How have questions helped you or someone you know unveil something in a new way?

Prayer

Tender God, you turn your ear to us and listen to our pleads, our heartbreak, and our hopes. Help us to offer this same gift of listening to others that we might honor their stories and help them know that their life matters. In these holy moments of telling and listening, may we encounter your presence and know you, ourselves, and the other more fully. In Jesus' name we pray. Amen.

4

Story Communities

For Lent this past year, my (Elaina's) congregation nixed Wednesday Lenten services and instead offered two small group opportunities. Coming out of the pandemic, from disconnection and isolation, we chose to focus on "Connections through Reflections." Our congregation was also celebrating our 150th anniversary and one of our goals was to create a book of vignettes to tell the stories of faith from people in the pew. Our Lenten small groups were intended to lay the groundwork for that book.

At one of our sessions, I offered these story prompts for people to respond to:

- What was the moment you realized the seriousness or felt the fear of the pandemic?
- What was a moment you felt hope in the pandemic?

We practiced contemplative listening, giving each person space to respond, offering a moment of silence between each speaker and not responding or asking questions of any storyteller.

The stories of realizing the seriousness of the pandemic were vivid. People reflected on major events being cancelled, schools shutting down and even church connections being lost. Someone shared about their pregnant daughter giving birth in a pandemic impacted hospital where families could not visit and be with someone they loved at such an important time. Stories were shared of kids who would take their place on opposite sides of the street to have a conversation at a safe distance — doing what they could to stay connected while obeying the rules they had been given. There was stress, frustration, fear and vulnerability in everyone's stories.

As the story circle ended, we reflected on the experience. One person said, "I know we were all going through this, but it felt really good to hear these stories. I don't feel as alone in what I had experienced." Another said, "We all shared our pain. We all shared something that broke our heart. And something about that felt good." When I asked the follow-up question of where we saw God in these stories, Mary said, "I didn't see God's presence at the time, but now I do." There was a sense of relief in her voice.

In our storytelling and our story listening, we met God. Not just in the stories, but in the present moment as we shared honestly and had our stories honored. We felt connected in our vulnerability and in our humanity. As Brené Brown, research social worker and author, says, "When we dare to drop the armor that protects us from feeling vulnerable, we open ourselves to the experiences that bring purpose and meaning to our lives." We will most often feel more connected through sharing our vulnerabilities than our successes.

Relationships are incarnational. In relationships marked by trust and honesty, where it is safe to be vulnerable and authentic, the love of God takes on flesh in the one we call friend. Relationships can be holy indeed as trusted companions become visible signs of God's invisible love.

We need community. We are hard wired for connection. The pandemic interruption to our social lives — and here I don't just mean missing parties or going out to a bar, but just being with family and dear friends — showed us just how much we universally need connection. We need each other.

We see that from the very start of creation. God did not want to be alone, and the animals, even in all their wonder, were not the companions that God was looking for. God was looking for us — people made to be the image of God in the world. Then, when the first person was created, God saw the human's need for companionship too. It wasn't good to be alone, for God or for us. Created in God's image, we were made for community and connection.

When we talk about story communities, we're talking about faith communities that make space for the type of storytelling and story listening that nurtures deeper interpersonal connections and faith. In story communities, we make sense of our stories together in light of God's story. We receive encouragement to keep putting one foot in front of another. We're reminded that we're loved in our imperfection and healed in our brokenness. We feel a little less alone in the world through our connection with others. Our convictions, compassion and bitterness can be changed by our neighbor's story. We meet God in the person before us and often receive the grace of God that is woven through our stories. Stories open our hearts to love and to God.

Making sense of our stories

There is power in getting to speak our stories aloud and have them received by a loving, listening presence. Often in telling our stories, we hear or discover some truth we might not have known if we kept the story inside us. In story communities, we can offer that kind of sacred space for one another.

Elena participates in her church's small group that is dedicated to understanding the complexity of racism and working on being anti-racist. She had grown-up in the church. Her grandfather was the former pastor at the church she now attends with her own children. For her day job, Elena works as a juvenile probation officer, a job she got into to serve and care for at-risk youth.

As time has gone on, however, she has questioned how her job might be more a part of the problem rather than the solution. During one meeting, Elena was telling part of her story and as she spoke, she started to see how what she believed about God and God's reign was part of what inspired her to go into her line of work. Her commitment to a more just world was born out of her faith. It's what she learned from Jesus. As she reflected on this, she said, "I never realized that until now." Elena understood her own life and story more deeply and could see how this story of our faith had shaped her passion and work. And she was blown away by the realization!

Elena was able to make sense of her story in a new and profound way in a story community where she was able to reflect on her life's unfolding.

Loved in our imperfection

In the Gospel of Matthew, as Jesus was dining at the house of Matthew the tax collector, the Pharisees challenged and critiqued Jesus for eating with sinners. Jesus said, "It is not the healthy who need a doctor, but the sick. But go and learn what this means, 'I desire mercy not sacrifice.' For I have not come to call the righteous, but the sinners." (Matthew 9:10-13) One of the reasons we are involved with faith communities is not because of our righteousness, it is because of our brokenness and need. In worship, we confess exactly that, and then, words of forgiveness are spoken over our lives. Thankfully, God loves us — even in our imperfection!

However, we spend a high percentage of our lives trying to prove our worthiness — even at church. God's love for us in our imperfection becomes tangible as story communities create safe places for our stories of vulnerability, and then respond to those stories with acceptance.

For several years at the congregation I (Elaina) serve, we have had lay storytellers during our Lenten midweek services. We usually develop a theme and then use story prompts around the theme to guide members of the congregation to tell their story in place of the sermon.

One time, Cynthia shared her story about being married to an alcoholic. She spoke of the challenges, her personal journey in setting boundaries and caring for herself, and the healing that happened over time. She shared about the strength she found in her faith. In her honesty and vulnerability, the time and space we shared was holy. At the end of worship that night, many people said, "I've known

Cynthia for years (like 30 years!) and I never knew that." They thanked her for her story, her courage and her witness.

For the listeners gathered that night, we all felt a little less alone all because one person shared her humanness, and thus, we heard permission to own and accept our humanity as well. We already loved Cynthia and her story of imperfection did not change that. In fact, our love for her grew deeper as we were let into this very personal part of her life. What we heard and what we felt is that we would be loved in our imperfection too. That was grace for all of us.

Story communities create space for imperfection, brokenness and vulnerability. The stories of our faith journey are not all sunshine, daffodils and blessing. We walk through very real valleys over which the shadow of death looms. We plead with God to answer the deepest prayers of our heart. We wrestle with God. These stories need sacred space. As we start to share them, we will find that we are often more connected through our vulnerability than through our success or strength. Simply admitting our humanness and letting go of our drive for worthiness and the walls we build to protect ourselves is an experience of grace.

Changed by our neighbor's story

When we listen to our neighbor's story, we can be changed by what we hear. Our neighbor's story can challenge our stereotypes and expectations and lead us to confession and repentance. Other people's stories can expand our worldview or undo a tightly held conviction. Through a neighbor's witness, we may see more clearly unjust systems. We can be changed by our neighbor's story. Another person's story can work in our hearts in deep ways.

At a recent workshop that I (Elaina) attended, Tecca, a Black woman, and I, a white woman, were paired together. She shared her story about working as a social worker at a juvenile correctional facility in a small town where most employees were white and often related to one another. Tecca told about a day when a white correctional officer was verbally abusive to one of the Black teenagers. The officer said awful things to the young man because he was drumming out a song beat on the wall. She articulated for us how the anger felt in her body, how she addressed the correctional officer, and then with fear and trembling, how she had marched to her superior to report the incident.

After hearing Tecca's story, it was then my assignment to share the story as if it were my own story within a larger group of four people. I was worried and distracted about getting the details right (and I didn't). What seemed most important was feeling the anger and heartbreak she experienced as well as the courage to step forward to address the abuse in that system. What was most important was experiencing at least some of the racism in my body and soul just as she did in hers, an experience that I have been protected from as a white woman. My worry about getting the details right distanced me from the fullness of her experience. Still, Tecca's story left a mark on my heart, especially as I tried to step into her life and not keep the story at a safe distance.

Story communities can bless people in various ways. Stories can take different forms, but when they are a priority, they shape how communities of faith form, grow and use their time together. In the following two communities, story is at the heart of their purpose and work.

The Hearth, creating story communities

The Hearth, based in Ashland, Oregon, sees their mission as transformational storytelling. The Hearth understands the power of stories to heal, connect, enrich and mobilize communities for good around the world. A storytelling project with the Mexican American Cultural Center in Austin, Texas, helped capture the stories of the suffering of undocumented people. They recorded and presented stories of kindness and generosity hidden in the sorrow after the mass shooting at Umpqua Community College in Oregon. In North Wales, they created a platform for people to hear the stories of refugees after the Brexit vote.

As part of a sabbatical, I (Elaina) worked on a Certificate in Community Storytelling through The Hearth. The training was led by Mark Yaconelli and consisted of two 3.5 day intensives, monthly webinars, a project and story coaching over the course of six months. The participants were from across the country and across disciplines, including church folks — pastors and lay leaders. There were also youth center workers caring for at-risk kids, scientists who were working on addressing climate change, a community activist addressing issues of gun violence, another community activist creating healing spaces after the devastation of wildfires, and university staff developing support programming for formerly incarcerated people attending college.

At the heart of our training was storytelling and story listening. Our trainer, Mark, gave us various story prompts, and broke us into small groups to share our stories. The story prompts included, "Tell a story of a tree that you loved," and "Talk about a moment of connection with a stranger." In one exercise, we considered the arc of our own life stories, and then with two listeners/witnesses, we each had fifteen minutes to share what was most essential about our life's unfolding. The story I previously shared about Tecca was another exercise in which we listened to another's story and then retold it as if it were our own.

It was a secular training, but I felt like I was in church throughout the training! Through storytelling and story listening, even on Zoom, we were in holy space. I became deeply connected to people who days before were strangers. I felt less alone as I heard my struggles reflected in other's stories. My classmates' desire to bring people together and work for healing and reconciliation stirred courage in me. The stories of the Native American women participants and their struggle for justice challenged and changed me. I was blown away by the sense of community and the powerful connections nurtured by storytelling and listening.

Gilead Church, a story community

The Chicago-based Gilead Church's website says, "We believe that every story, at its heart, is a God story." Their worship life manifests this conviction. When people arrive for worship, each person is handed a small slip of paper with a story prompt that fits the day's theme. A story prompt might be, "I felt fully seen when ____," or "I (finally) felt at home when ___." They fill in their two to three sentence story and submit their answer anonymously, if they choose to. There's safety in the anonymity. As worship begins, the pastor reads these mini-stories and the community gets a sense of who is in the room.

Each service also has someone who shares a more fully developed, personal story related to the theme. When they are done with the story, the leader says, "The word of God for the people of God," to which the congregation responds, "Thanks be to God." The acclamation affirms that the story tells us something of God, of what it means to be human and of the reality of suffering and grace woven through the stories of our lives. From there, the services fall into a rhythm that might be a bit more familiar — readings, sermon, prayers and communion. Grounded in story, Gilead Church proclaims the incarnational nature of God. They see and put into practice the conviction that our lives are a revelation.

Pastor Rebecca Anderson says Gilead Church believes "true stories save lives." She explains that many in the Gilead community have experienced church in ways that have not been welcoming to their story, or at least some pieces of it. The freedom and invitation to share stories that were previously unwelcomed and then to hear it pronounced "The word of God for the people of God," can be a holy moment — for many, a moment of real grace. "True stories save lives" is also experienced in receiving stories. Honesty and vulnerability are welcome, and through those things, connections and intimacy are nurtured.

Stories connect us to each other

I hope each reader has experienced the power of connection that can happen through sharing and receiving stories. There is some science behind what we intuitively know through these experiences.

Princeton psychology and neuroscience professor, Uri Hasson, has studied what happens in our brain as we hear a story. Our brain waves actually start to synchronize with the storyteller. Professor Hasson and his research team set up an experiment that recorded the brain activity of one storyteller and one story listener. Sure enough, the brain wave patterns started to sync. The story listener's brain activity started to mirror that of the storyteller. ("How Stories Connect and Persuade Us: Unleashing the Brain Power of Narrative")

In addition to brain waves mirroring each other, the "love hormone," oxytocin, is released as we listen to stories. Something physically changes in us as we listen. That unseen something connects us.

Through storytelling and story listening, a "we" is formed out of a bunch of "I's." Through story, a group of individuals are drawn into relationship with one another.

In the Lenten small groups that we started this chapter with, people in community together shared a sacred story. Those connections were nurtured and deepened through sharing their personal stories. Had the sacred container for such story sharing not been offered, people would have held on to their stories and felt more isolated because of it.

The participants in the Hearth's Community Storytelling Training only had personal stories to draw them together. There was no common faith conviction — no shared sacred story. But as people shared their lives and received each other's stories, authentic community was formed.

For Gilead Church, the stories and belovedness of each person are welcomed and celebrated. As the welcome and celebration happens for someone, it happens for others who witness it. Each story creates sacred space for another story. Something greater yet starts to form — a "we," a collective identity, a community.

Stories connect us. Communities dedicated to sharing stories nurture connection and intimacy between individuals. They create sacred space for life to be shared and received gracefully. From here, a "we" is shaped and formed.

Stories connect us to God

Storytelling and story listening put us on holy ground. They put us in God's presence.

Stories help us see God as an actor in our story. As people in Lenten small groups told stories, Mary could name where she saw God's faithful care and presence. As Elena, reflected on her life's story, she realized how her faith and career were intertwined, so that her career started to feel more like a vocation. We can see currents of grace, God's activity and deeper meaning woven in the stories of our lives.

Stories connect us in the moment of sharing. The intimacy shared becomes incarnational. The storyteller and story listener become visible signs of God's invisible love. In that moment, we know once again that we are not alone. That is an experience of God discovered in community.

Finally, when we can open ourselves to vulnerability, we open ourselves to meaning and purpose. Even more, we open ourselves to God. When we can tell the story of being fully human — including our fears, our longings, our heartbreak and our brokenness — we name our need for God. Sometimes, in just the naming, the honesty and the armor falling away, we receive God's loving response of grace and mercy in and through one another.

For Reflection and Discussion

As you finish this chapter and reflect, use the resources below for personal reflection or, even better, to discuss this material with others in a team or small group.

Scripture

In the same way, though there are many of us, we are one body in Christ, and individually we belong to each other... Love should be shown without pretending. Hate evil, and hold on to what is good. Love each other like the members of your family. Be the best at showing honor to each other. (Romans 12:5, 9-10 CEB)

Questions

1. Romans 12 begins a section of Paul's letter to the Romans that applies the gospel to the life of the faith community. Where have you experienced authentic, gospel love in community? How does love happen in the faith community in which you participate?

2. Share a story of a time you experienced a deep sense of connectedness in community. How did it happen? How did it make you feel?

continued ...

3. Think about your closest friends. How has sharing stories moved beyond just information to creating more meaningful relationships?

4. Think about experiences of community you have had – inside and outside of church life. How have you seen or experienced stories used well to nurture community? Where did they happen and what made those times so significant?

5. How does your congregation currently use stories? What are three things you'd like to try to see if you can strengthen the story sharing in your faith community?

Prayer

God, Story Creator, nurture among us a community that welcomes stories of joy, hope, doubt, loss, and suffering. Bind us together in our storytelling and story listening. Help us hold stories, and the people who tell them, with tender care. Use this holy work, to inspire our faith, for certainly in the listening and the telling, we will encounter you. We pray this in the name of the One who speaks your word of love to us, Jesus Christ, our Lord. Amen.

Conclusion

Stories are simply life happening. Everything we live and experience happens within a story. For faith communities to be relevant, they simply need to find ways to make stories be at the center of what they do and make the connections between who God is and the stories we live and share. In a sense, once we get deeper than chit-chat then huge spaces open up for meaningful and exciting connections.

To help you with this work, we have included a section after this conclusion that we call "Tactics." It is a bit of an appendix with lots of ways that we have done this work or seen others do it as well. Use that section to get ideas and try things. Some ideas are for small groups. Some work in larger settings like worship. Most can be adapted to work in either setting. It is far from exhaustive — create your own ways that work for you and the people with whom you share your faith life.

In this book we have come at stories from four places. Each angle offers something important to the way we share stories and how we make sense of them. So as we finish, let's take a brief moment to review in the hope that it will help you frame your own storytelling work.

God's story

Remember that this is all happening within God's story. Every faith community has some grounding that joins them — a narrative that is bigger than any of us. For Christians, that narrative is about God, the Story Creator — the one who made the world and then has come out of love to be a part of it in the life, death and resurrection of Jesus. As both author and actor, the crucified and risen Christ shapes how we see God continuing to be involved in loving and healing our world. It forms the umbrella underneath which all our stories live and breathe.

As you do this work, be sure to connect God's story to the stories you elicit from the people you live in community with. Knowing the biblical story will help everyone see how God's stories continue to be written in the fabric of our lives. Knowing God's story well will help each of us have benchmarks to help us make sense of our experiences.

Concerning God's story, do people know the biblical story well? Do they see it as a story of love and grace? Do what you can to increase biblical literacy and fluency — especially biblical storytelling. These form the framework for a community grounded in God's love and grace. And connecting God's story to the stories of people provides a framework for their faith life. That is an amazing gift!

The storyteller

Then we explored the importance of the storyteller. Without the story being told, all of this comes to a screeching halt. Any one of us can assume this role. Each of us brings the life we have to the table. It is out of that life that we share our stories as co-writers within God's great story. Each life is uniquely positioned to tell its story like no one else can. It is our story to tell. How we tell it and what we share from it can help us make sense of our own journey, connect it to the larger work of God and be a gift that helps those who hear it discover something about their own journey.

Help each person to be a storyteller and encourage them to share their stories. Give people prompts. Model it for them. Visit them individually and listen to them when they are not in a larger group. They may feel safer talking to a single listener. Then offer them opportunities to share in larger group settings with your sincere encouragement, "That story was amazing. Others need to hear what you just shared with me." Help people sort through their lives looking for joys and celebrations, sorrows and struggles, times of healing or reconciliation, and more. Anything we can do to help people see and articulate their own story is a gift.

The story listener

That brings us to the work of being a story listener. Story listening is so important that, as we wrote this book, it was a coin flip as to whether to deal with story listener or storyteller first. Both need each other and are essential.

Generous, effective listening is an act of love. A good story listener will ask, draw out and make space for the storyteller to share and share well. So, learning to ask good questions, creating safe space and being open to receive stories are important. If you want to do this well, remind members of the faith community of good practices for listening and encourage them to use them when they are gathered and in their daily lives and relationships. Teaching people to be curious, receptive and skilled at listening will change the character of the gathered community.

When we listen well, we make space for those who tell their stories to risk digging deeper and discover new things. At the same time, in the hearing we learn more about the truth of life, not only that of the storyteller, but the truth about all our lives. That means you don't always need to say anything to learn something about your own story. The depth of hearing someone else's story can touch us right at the core and lead us to discover something about ourselves at the same time.

Story communities

Finally, faith communities that commit to this as a regular and central part of their shared life together will find connections formed in ways that are surprising and lasting, inspiring and healing. It is easy to become disconnected when our shared life is shallow, but we find deeper connections being made and lasting relationships formed when we allow ourselves to truly be vulnerable and touched by each other's stories. The deepest bonds of life happen when sharing is personal and genuine, and hearts are touched. Find ways to share your stories in community and your congregation will never be the same, and neither will the people who are part of it.

Remember that your faith community is already a story community on its way. Find ways to grow this so it is not limited to something that certain people do because they are considered to be better storytellers than others. If you want stories to be widely shared and valued, you are not just teaching a few interested folks to do this, you are gradually shaping the culture of the entire faith community in which you participate. Moving from the few to a larger "we" takes time and being intentional, persistent, observant and patient. When things go well, celebrate them and offer encouragement. When something doesn't go as well, be gracious and find ways to learn from the experience. Over time, congregations will do well to create a culture where the biblical story is known, told well and told often. As that culture takes root and grows, the congregation will carefully make space for new stories to be added to the community's narrative as they are told and heard by people of all ages, perspectives, abilities and life experiences.

A final word and sending

We want to finish with a word of encouragement. It wasn't that long ago that people thought big, mega-churches were going to rule the future. But as generations shifted and the pandemic wreaked havoc on all aspects of our shared lives, it has become clear that the future is not as simple or as clear as some of the pundits and experts thought. Many people now value less big and bold and instead yearn for space for meaningful relationships and intimacy — hungering for deeper connections and to know and be authentically known.

Learning to tell God's story and your story and to hear the stories of others will remain at the heart of at least one important form of Christian community in the years to come — the story community. Many of these story-centered faith communities will flourish and be places of deep connections between God and God's people. Stories are who we are. Stories remind us of where we come from and where we are heading. In a world filled with infinite mysteries, those are amazing and important gifts.

So, go with God and know God goes with you as well!

Tactics for Moving Beyond Chit-Chat

Chit-chat is natural and easy for most of us. We have been trained to ask the same questions over and over, to respond "fine" when asked how we are doing, and to cover many of the same topics with the people we see. Repetitive but easy and safe – that's how we mostly play the game.

But deeper sharing comes when we are intentional about the conversations we have and the ways that we pay attention to one another. This is true of our individual lives. All of us can gain skill and be more open to listening to the deeper and more meaningful aspects of one another's lives.

But it is even more true for communities of faith. Leaders can lead by modeling as they tell stories. Leaders can lead by asking others good questions and listening to people as they respond. Leaders can lead by finding ways to share the floor with those whose voices have much to share but are perhaps quieter for one reason or another.

That's why this section is included here. The ideas below are various simple but powerful tactics to help people identify their stories and find ways to share them with their faith community. Some are more introspective first to allow people to reflect on the stories they have to share. Others are more interactive to provide a platform for people to share the stories that mean the most to them in their life journey.

Storytellers at Midweek Services

An opportunity for story sharing can happen in the midweek services that many congregations have for seasons like Advent and Lent. These are a great chance to hear from people in the pews, in part because the atmosphere is often more intimate and feels safer in size as people share – sometimes for the first time in a public way.

In preparation for the season, prepare story prompts that match the theme or assigned readings. These may come from the journal prompts that follow or be constructed around a theme. In the weeks leading up to the season, share those story prompts with the congregation and seek out one storyteller to share each week. The story can be shared in place of a sermon.

One year, our Lenten theme was "Broken Hallelujah." The theme was woven into each week's liturgy. However, we did not utilize a storyteller every week. The series developed like in the table on the next page.

This is just an example of what was done in one setting during one Lent. Think up your own themes and prompts and enjoy trying to develop a series of themes that connect well and where stories are at the center. Invite people to reflect on stories and agree to share during one of the weeks. Then help them tell stories and listen to one another as the stories are shared.

Brokenness of...	Story Prompt
Sin	Ash Wednesday. No storyteller.
Faith	Share about a time you had a crisis of faith or your faith felt broken. What did doubt feel like? What did you learn about yourself or God during this time? Where did you find your "Hallelujah" in the brokenness?
Mind, Body, or Spirit	Share about a time you felt broken in mind, body, and/or spirit. Where did you find hope or patience in the suffering? How did God uphold you? Where did you find your "hallelujah" in the brokenness?
Addiction	Share a story of addiction. What was the struggle like? What "need" was the addiction trying to fulfill? What did rock bottom look like? What did you learn about yourself or God? Where or how did you discover your "hallelujah" in the brokenness?
Relationships	Share a story about a broken relationship. What felt irreparable? Did reconciliation happen? How did you learn to forgive? Where did you find your "Hallelujah" in the brokenness?
War and Violence	Prayer Service Only. No storyteller
Justice	Good Friday, No storyteller.

Journaling for Lent

Many people need help getting started as they reflect on their faith stories. Ask some people without a prompt and you will often get a deer in the headlights look. So specific prompts and questions can help people focus and find an entry point to identifying their own story.

Help your community "listen to their lives" with a journaling discipline for Lent. Parishioners can be encouraged to use their journals in a way that best suits them. For example, people could keep a gratitude journal listing the gifts of each day. Journals can be used for writing about the day's unfolding. Using an examen type reflection, writers could reflect on the consolations or desolations of each day. Or journals could be used to respond to story prompts such as the ones that follow. Journals are for personal reflection only and are not meant to be collected or shared at the end of the season.

So here are 40 Journal Prompts for 40 Days of Lent

1. What is a childhood memory of church?
2. Write a story of an early experience of God.
3. When did your faith come alive or become real to you?
4. Write about a time when you had doubts or wrestled with God.
5. Write about a time when you heard God speak.
6. When did you experience God's presence in nature?
7. Write a story about when you realized the seriousness of the pandemic.
8. Write a story about when you experienced a moment of grace and hope in the pandemic.

9. Read 2 Corinthians 12:9. Reflect on the text in your journal.
10. What renews your spirit? What feeds your soul?
11. What Bible story is most meaningful to you?
12. When did you experience God's presence in a crisis or a challenge?
13. Write a story about a time you felt deeply connected to someone.
14. Write a story of about the kindness of a stranger.
15. When did someone else's story challenge you? Did it lead to transformation or repentance?
16. Write about a time you felt God's silence or experienced "the dark night of the soul."
17. What is God teaching you now?
18. Write about a time it was hard to love someone.
19. Write a story about a time it was difficult to forgive.
20. Write a story about a time you had to ask for forgiveness.
21. Read 1 Peter 5:7. Reflect on the text in your journal.
22. When did God surprise you with a new opportunity or possibility?
23. How has God made you unique? What gifts has God blessed you with?
24. When have you felt humbled by how God used your gifts to love and serve?
25. Write a story of a time you felt like an outsider.

26. Write about a time when practicing vulnerability led to a gift of grace or wholeness.
27. Let your grief speak. Tell its story.
28. Read John 16:33. Reflect on the text in your journal.
29. What brings you joy?
30. What gives you hope?
31. What is God calling you to?
32. When have you felt angry with God?
33. When has God answered a prayer?
34. What is the deepest prayer of your heart today?
35. Where does your greatest joy meet the world's deepest need?
36. When have you experienced listening as an act of love?
37. Write a story of when you were in need of healing in body, mind, or spirit.
38. Read Philippians 4:8. Reflect on the text in your journal.
39. What do you believe about God?
40. What is the hardest thing for you to face right now?

Story Circles, Contemplative Listening, and Group Spiritual Direction

Secular settings may call it a story circle, while faith communities might call it contemplative listening. By either name, the practice is similar. The process allows a group of people to form a circle within which a person can safely share a story and it can simply be received graciously by those who hear.

Story Circle

A group of people is gathered and provided a story prompt. Each person gets a turn to share. In larger groups, a time limit may need to be enforced. If someone is not prepared to share, they may pass, but after everyone has had a turn, the invitation to share returns to them and they can either accept or decline. Different than a conversation, participants are asked not to respond to each other's stories. With this format, there is no cross talk and no interrupting or hijacking someone's story. Story listeners receive the gift of the storyteller.

Contemplative Listening

With contemplative listening, the process is similar in that each person gets a turn to share and participants are asked not to respond to each other's stories. Added dimensions to contemplative listening include beginning and ending in prayer, listening deeply and prayerfully from one's heart center, keeping silence between each story, and being attentive to God's presence in the story and in the process. Listeners give up the need to fix or advise the storyteller. When the speaker is done, they may say, "That is all I have to say." Contemplative listening can be done in response to a story prompt or a poem, prayer, or quote. For our purposes, it is a process of prayerfully sharing and receiving stories.

Group Spiritual Direction

This format takes contemplative listening one step further. In this process, a speaker has ten to fifteen minutes to share their story or struggle without interruption. When the storyteller is done speaking, the group remains silent for several minutes so that participants can listen for what the Spirit has to say through them. Listeners than share with the speaker how they heard the Spirit speaking through them. It's a different kind of listening and responses should not proceed from our own need or ego, but through a holy listening of the Spirit's voice. Again, the comments should be reflective and supportive – not critical or corrective. When the sharing is done, silence is kept once again, and the speaker is held in silent prayer by the group's participants. The next speaker starts the process over again. This level of sharing is more interactive in ways that increase vulnerability than the above two circles, and it may be best to have a facilitator with more skills, perhaps a trained spiritual director.

Stories of Faith from the Pew

Congregational history is its own doorway into stories. In fact, the history of the congregation is one expression of our collective story, one that we all share in some way. This can be done any time, but church anniversaries are a great chance to do this work in a focused and elevated way. The congregations the authors serve have each celebrated 150th and 140th anniversaries during the time we have been writing this book. Each congregation was formed by groups of immigrants who had come here in the 1800s. Each place has books, files and boxes of records, picture, newspaper clippings, membership rosters, and more. Stories of building the facilities, financing the work, educating the next generations, and more are all buried in there.

Of course, we are curious about the faith of those who walked through the doors over the past years. That story is sometimes missed because it was not the kind of thing that was likely to be recorded in the annual meeting minutes both then and now. So, using an anniversary as a chance to share faith stories adds a layer that may or may not be clearly present in what we have received from our predecessors.

One offering for an anniversary celebration can be a book of vignettes that seeks to capture the stories of faith from the people in the pew, many of which will come from older members who can fill in faith stories that go back decades! The congregation can be provided story prompts and then invited to write a paragraph or two in response to prompts that speak to them. Then, compile these stories in a book and add it to the materials that are passed forward to those who will follow.

The story prompts could include the following (and many more!):

- What is a childhood memory of our church?

- Tell a story of an early experience of God.

- Tell a story of a favorite [enter church name] tradition (may be of a different era).

- Tell a story of when you experienced God through worship or a ministry experience at church. What was a holy moment you experienced here in this congregation?

- Tell the story of one of our dearly departed saints. What made them special? How did God use them to touch your life?

- Tell a story when you felt nurtured by love as a part of this congregation.

- Tell a story of when you felt that God was using your unique gifts to serve with hope at church and beyond. Tell a story when you served outside our church walls.

- Tell a story about a difficult time in your life or a difficult time while you have been a part of this congregation? Where/how did you see God in the difficulty?

- Because of the timing of anniversaries now, pandemic questions may be especially interesting to those who read this years from now. This is a reminder that sometimes there are specific events that may be relevant to this moment in time and unique to your time and/or place. The pandemic is just an example. Perhaps your church was impacted by a hurricane or tornado or your town was impacted by some serious event. Questions we used were:

    - Tell a story about the moment you realized the seriousness of the pandemic. Tell a story about when you experienced a moment of grace and hope in the pandemic.

    - What was it like to worship and meet online using livestreaming, Zoom, etc.?

- Finally, for you, what story of faith or experience at this congregation longs to be told?

Interviews

Conducting an interview during a public forum or in worship can help people share their stories more clearly and with confidence The presence of a supportive person who serves as interviewer gives the storyteller the clear sense that they are not up there alone. Plus, the interviewer gives a structure to the telling – the person knows they can stay on track and be clear and will have help doing so. If things move off the rails a bit, there is someone they trust there to help.

Two kinds of interviews that I have found helpful are story interviews and vocational interviews.

Story interviews are more specific – they connect thematically with the messages that shape sermons and worship. That means the stories are less general and more targeted. I may invite someone to share a story about their struggles and how they encountered God in them when the scriptures for a given week focus on struggle. The same story may not be as helpful on another week.

Vocational interviews are useful in a more general way. Anyone can be invited to do a vocational interview at any time. They are simple in format and ask people to share how they spend a part of their life working and how they see it connecting to God's desires for the world.

Story Interviews

One method that has borne much fruit is the use of interviews in public settings like worship. In all of our ministries we are likely to find stories and experiences that are deep, profound and worthy of more attention.

At the same time, many people who have a story which should be heard by many, are not wired to get up and give a talk to a group of people. Shyness and genuine fear prevent them from giving anything that resembles public speaking. Sadly, that means many stories never find their way to the audience that would be blessed to hear them.

Bar stools can be a great tool for this. They elevate the speaker so they can be seen by the group, but allow them to sit which may make them more comfortable. Instead of people needing to plan and give something that felt like a speech, they could simply join the interviewer/preacher on a stool up front and have a conversation that would be overheard by a larger group. Take on the role of Oprah or Stephen Colbert and simply welcome them and walk them through their story as your guest.

The results have been amazing. Changing the feel of the time from speech to conversation has opened the door for many people to share. And as some have shared, seeing the sharing has opened the door for others to be open to sharing – a sort of "I could do that…" environment has emerged.

The goal is for everyone who does an interview to feel glad to have the chance. Always meet with them ahead of time and agree on the questions. Because this is not a "gotcha" new environment, the goal is for everyone to share the story well and no one to risk looking bad. We want a mix of safety and authenticity for everyone who dives in.

When you meet to prepare for this, you already know some of their story – that's why you invited them to do an interview in worship. But letting them share in one spot what they have to say helps both of us focus on the story at hand. There is usually some theme in the message that week where this story becomes the showing of reality – and it is almost always best to have the story told by a participant rather than third hand by the preacher. Then you think about questions that will guide the conversation on Sunday morning when we have the interview. Always outline the questions with them and share them before the interview. The goal of the questions is to make the story feel more conversational and keep the teller at ease. And knowing them ahead means the storyteller can focus on the sharing of the story – not worrying about what surprise might come up along the way.

When the actual time for the interview arrives, have the storyteller introduce themselves by asking them to share a bit. Then invite them to share the story that prompted your invitation. During the interview, you may say a bit here and there in an "active listening" mode but usually try to let them tell their own story with as little input as possible. Just use the agreed on questions to guide the flow and keep it feeling conversational. The last question can usually be some interpretive faith/theology question like, "Where did you see God at work in this?" or "What did you learn through this experience that you can share with us?" The goal here is to move from story to theology in some way. The interview doesn't have to do all of that work as these usually are to closing part of sermon time and a preacher can help put a bow on this, always without showing up the storyteller but by lifting that up as a gift to the community.

Try to keep interviews to under ten minutes. That's a lot of time for a person to be known, share their story and do a bit of reflection on it. While almost every interview has been surprising in some way, they have always been positive experiences and the affirmation from others who listened as they shared is always encouraging. This has been the easiest way for new voices to find their way in front of the congregation.

Vocational Interviews

Another kind of interview is a vocational interview. We first learned of these through the Theology of Work Project, an online project to connect the biblical story to the ongoing work of God's people in daily life. You can find out more about this group at www.theologyofwork.org where you will find numerous other resources related to how people live out their vocation as a Christian.

Of course, for many people, the work they do is a huge part of their life. In fact, many people would identify themselves by what they do ("Hi. I'm Bill. I teach 8th grade science."). Our work is a huge venue for our lives and a place where much of our story takes place.

A vocational interview is a chance for a person to share one angle on their life story. When I do these, I invite someone to share in front of the congregation. The format is simple and consistent:

- Introduce yourself
- What kind of work do you do?
- When it goes well, what does God hope happens through your work?
- What challenges do you face doing this?
- How can we pray for you?

A vocational interview is usually short and lasts three or four minutes. But the interview gives people a chance to reflect on their work through the lens of faith. It also helps all who hear it reflect on their work and faith too. These are a great way to deepen everyone's stories and how we all see God in the midst of the ordinary.

Video Interviews

We mentioned anniversaries as doorways in a tactic above. Often, as part of that work, a committee is formed to oversee the theme and activities for the celebration. An excellent place to mine for stories is to invite some of the long-time members to remember things that were significant to them in the life of the congregation.

This is a great place to use video (as are many other situations) as you can talk to the people when it works for everyone, no one has to be up speaking in public, and the video gives access to even shut-in members to be interviewed. And if the questions are structured ahead, as they should be, even youth can do the interviews and use video to record them. Give everyone who is interviewed the same questions – prompts to share stories. Then share the videos as a whole or edit them based on the questions in a series of videos – each with material from one of the questions and all the respondents.

The final videos can then be used in worship. It is a simple way for some of our older members to speak comfortably and be heard. It gives voice to the stories they have and rekindle memories from their past. And a bonus is that the first people to hear each of these stories can be from any segment of the church, even people in their teens, and the stories can move across two or three generations as intergenerational relationships are expanded. And because the video will be edited and shaped – everyone will look good in the final product. People can share with less anxiety about speaking to a group and without worrying about "messing up." Everyone wins.

Be Creative!

This section on tactics is far from exhaustive. It's just some of the things we as the authors of this book have done and seen fruit from. Much of this doesn't even take tactics like the ones listed above – it just takes a few basic skills and intentionality. Get people talking about something in particular that goes deeper than chit-chat and they will go beyond chit-chat. It really is that simple.

Getting beyond chit-chat is a meaningful and important aspect of renewing the life of a congregation and the people who make it up. Faith stories spawn both more faith stories and also provide raw material for the Holy Spirit to do the work of giving new faith.

So be creative and enjoy telling and listening to stories of faith and see what God will do with it!